Sydney Prior Hall

Sketches from an Artist's Portfolio

Sydney Prior Hall

Sketches from an Artist's Portfolio

ISBN/EAN: 9783742844897

Manufactured in Europe, USA, Canada, Australia, Japa

Cover: Foto ©Thomas Meinert / pixelio.de

Manufactured and distributed by brebook publishing software
(www.brebook.com)

Sydney Prior Hall

Sketches from an Artist's Portfolio

"Waiting for the bear"

THE PRINCE OF WALES IN RUSSIA.

(see page 30)

FROM AN

ARTIST'S PORTFOLIO

SYDNEY P. HALL

London

SAMPSON LOW, MARSTON, LOW, AND SEARLE

CROWN BUILDINGS, 188, FLEET STREET

1875

LIST OF ILLUSTRATIONS.

FRANCE. 1870.

ARREST OF THE ARTIST.

ARRIVED at Holsheim, we asked at once for the Quartier Général. An old man in broad felt hat, and his daughter in a head-dress of broad ribbon, led us to a pretty little villa, at the gate of which was a sentinel. Passing him, we found some soldiers seated at a garden-table before the door. My friend stated who we were and what we wanted. An officer was sent for, who spoke English as well as I could. I asked him, first, whether we could get on to Strasbourg, and, secondly, whether, in default of this, I might be allowed to follow the army as an artist. He spoke a word to the general, who sat inside at dinner, and returned. "You must leave this place immediately. You must not stay an instant!" He beckoned to a trooper, who mounted his horse and loaded his pistol, and ordered him to see us back to Holsheim. I raised my hat to the officer, a courtesy which he did not return, and we moved on.

On our way back under guard I trudged along with chin on chest, very downcast at such treatment; but the Doctor was jovial, never happier in his life. He stuck his hat on one side, flung his coat over his arm, put his hands in his pockets, offered brandy to the dragoon, slung his leg on the saddle-bow, and, finally, finding walking too slow for him, broke into a Caffir-like trot. Then the dragoon was after him in a twinkling. It was a comic scene — the Englishman loping along the line like a rabbit, offering a splendid mark to the dragoon's pistol, the dragoon spurring, his horse buck-jumping, his accoutrements rattling. The din behind him was too much even for the Doctor, who, suddenly recollecting that a flesh wound behind is hard to heal, and by no means honourable, stopped.

AT METZ, BEFORE THE STATUE OF MARSHAL NEY.

AT the end of the square in Metz stands Ney's statue, grim, defiant, musket in hand. All around were the picturesque country carts, the horses unharnessed, and quietly munching the hay which they had just brought into the town. About the statue of the Marshal were grouped soldiers of every diversity of uniform, looking up admiringly at the "bravest of the brave," wondering, maybe, whether this war would produce another Duke of Elchingen to lead desperate attacks and defend as desperate retreats. While I sketched, stared at and suspected, I saw the *patron* of the Hotel de France, Nancy, where I had stayed. I hailed him, anxious to claim acquaintance with a Frenchman. He recognized me, but passed by me quickly, only saying, "Toujours travailler, Monsieur! Quel joli talent!"

FRANCE, 1870.

"UNDER FIRE."

THERE'S the queer little counter, in the *Comte de Toulouse*, Versailles, behind which sits Sidonie darning her *serviettes*. I have seen the sacred counter invaded by a ruthless German, who found the position a very hot one to hold, he was *under such a fire* from Sidonie's eyes. Then there's the funny spiral staircase up and down which the *garçon* goes. I dislike that *garçon*, in spite of his spotless, highly-decorated shirts and absence of waistcoat. Yet I believe him to be an honest *garçon*, and I know that he loves Sidonie to distraction. Look at him crouching like a jaguar at the head of the couple behind the counter, war to the knife blazing in his fiery eyes. Ah! they trifle with an honest heart! His sole wish is the sudden death of the *patron*, his sole ambition to lead Sidonie to the altar, and instal her mistress of the *Comte de Toulouse*. Till then he is content patiently to *wait*.

THE BABE AND THE BUGBEAR.

ON the brink of the Bassin de Neptune, Versailles, a burly Landwehr man stoops and holds treasonous communication with a tiny little French maid. The Landwehr man (Bismarck, may be—the bugbear of French babes) and the tiny French maid have established an *entente cordiale*. Thus one touch of nature makes the whole world kin.

FRANCE, 1870.

FOUR SKETCHES OF VERSAILLES.

I confess I have made these sketches for want of something better to do.

There are days in the long monotony of a siege when even a special artist must be idle.

To sit down quietly and draw a palace dedicated "À TOUTES LES GLOIRES DE LA FRANCE," with "Le Grand Monarque" in the foreground, while the Red-Cross flag waves over all, and the Place d'Armes below is filled with German artillery, seems a cold-blooded thing to do.

The artistic *espion* cannot be suffered to take a holiday in peace. As he sketches a bit of the park, the quaintly-shaped trees on the terraces, the fountains, or the *tapis vert*, and the canal beyond, all sunny, autumnal tinted, and still, an aged couple near him under an umbrella whispers one to the other loud enough for him to hear: "Ils (*i. e.* the Germans) ont des gens de talent partout; il tire le plan du parc."

The fountains lay for the most part sulky and *en deuil*. Once or twice they were made to play, but they did it with a bad grace. Home said he heard a German, very drunk, and reeling against a grating, say plaintively, as he looked towards the fountains, "Les grands oiseaux! ça ne va pas. Les grands oiseaux! Bon jour, les grands oiseaux."

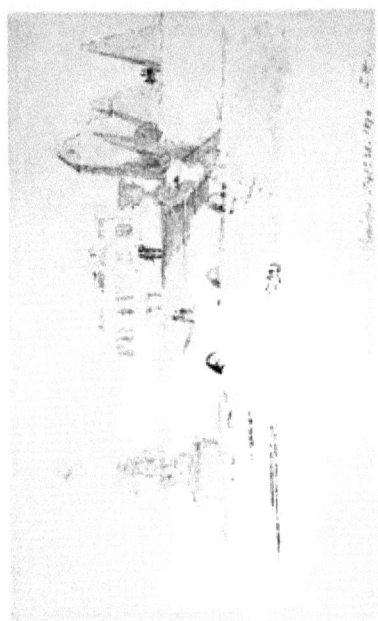

FRANCE, 1870.

ST. CLOUD.

In these bowery pleasances all is changed. The Prussian-tents swagger where the Empress's most select coffee-tables used to stand. Of the trees, which no man dared profane, a junker has made a wigwam. The ugliest German resounds in the home of the smoothest French. The *Follet* is banished, the sour *Zeitung* has come, and the *toppo* is changed for the *pickelhaube*.

LULU'S EISENBAHN.

THE playground of the Prince Imperial at St. Cloud is in as thorough ruin as the big palace close by. A miniature railway, with all its belongings, station, viaduct, sidings, points, and signals, all torn up, demolished, as if they had been real means to bring troops to the relief of Paris: A big German pioneer, with one foot on the embankment, the other on the path beneath, trying the toy switch : A German Gulliver in a French Lilliput.

This is Lulu's Eisenbahn.

Outpost in the Park of St Cloud
(In front of troops)

1e Compagnie 38 Regiment

Les bois enverbala St Cloud

The German Gulliver in the French Lilliput

FRANCE, 1870.

A SOLDIER'S CHRISTMAS TREE;
OR, CHRISTMAS-EVE AT MONTMORENCY.

AT Montmorency, while staying in the *Villa Archibald Forbes*, I found one of the many deserted houses which lie around Paris, and, its situation being a good one for the purpose, it had been occupied by the Germans, and to a certain extent turned into a fortified post, the windows being packed with turf. On the upper floor was what used to be the billiard-room; the table, and cues, and scoring-board were still there, but the table had been turned into a bed, and the cues had been used for pinning some gabions together which had been stuffed into a hole in the roof where a French shell had been "*pocketed.*" The soldiers had been keeping Christmas, and had improvised a Christmas-tree of a peculiarly grim kind. A pile of needle-guns, with candles stuck on the bayonet points, did duty for the fir-tree, while the men sat round drinking toasts: "Here's to home again;" "Nach Paris;" and others.

ON THE ROAD TO PARIS.

THE next morning the "some time or other" of our hopeful companion had come, and the weather had cleared; so we started upon the road, tolerably refreshed by our night's rest, and not without hopes that the heat of the sun might prove sufficient to dry our still damp clothes. That morning's ride to Clermont was along a road which showed constant traces of war. Dead horses lay here and there in all stages of decomposition, the deserted bivouacs by the roadside were dotted with the holes cut for the fires, and strewn with bones, offal, and broken bottles. The furrows and hollows were filled with muddy rain-water, the telegraph wires cut and trailing on the ground, the roads and paths trampled and cut up, the trees felled. It was a most desolate scene, and gave me, for one, an idea of what a destructive process the mere march of an army must be. We saw here and there barrows marking the burial-places of the dead soldiers, the victims, I presume, of sickness and disease, as there has been no fighting about this part; and there they are likely to stand until, some few centuries hence, some inquisitive antiquary will dig into their depths and prove to the satisfaction of the world, and himself in particular, that the bones were the bones of the ancient Goths, and the metal buttons a primitive kind of coin.

FRANCE, 1870.

UNDER THE MISTLETOE BOUGH.

It was about Christmas time, 1870, when Mr. John Furley induced me to jog along with him to Beaugency, 100 miles, in a limber waggon filled with stores for the wounded there. The bunches of mistletoe in the roadside apple-trees recalled the season. The roast beef of Old England was *not recalled* by the dead half-flayed, frozen horses lying here and there *under the mistletoe bough*—a banquet for a crowd of crows. They had enough and to spare—so much the better; for the soil lay very lightly over the poor fellow buried in the ditch, the twisted twigs and a piece of paper for tombstone and epitaph.

BURIED QUICK AND UNBURIED DEAD.

The sketch was made while I was staying with Mr. Archibald Forbes at Margency, and he and I had hard work to excogitate a ghastly title for a ghastly sketch. It was he who succeeded in finding this. The scene itself was bad enough, but what made it more ghastly still was that close to the bivouac of the dead lay a bivouac of the living. The straw that the men had carried with them was to line round rifle-pits they had dug in the field some half-dozen yards apart, and in each hole nestled six or eight for warmth, their bodies buried, their faces and bayonets gleaming over the brink of their shooting-graves. Who was it sowed dragons' teeth, and from the seed sprang armed men?

The scene put one in mind of the legend. Why was the hill bristling with armed men? Over the valley glared the electric light of Fort Nogent, and should the French sally down, these buried dragons' teeth would spring up as armed men to receive them. It was a terrible service, made more terrible still by the neighbourhood of those unburied dead.

Study for Mistletoe Sprigs. Christmas France 1870

'Burili quick and ashamed dead' — "Schützen graben."

FRANCE, 1870.

RUINS OF ST. CLOUD.

We turned to our left, and the basin of a fountain lay before us. We rode up to it, and then to the right, at the end of an avenue of marble statues, flowers, and orange-trees, stood—no, tottered—the charred ruins of St. Cloud. I found two officers, with whom I was destined to form a closer acquaintance, sitting at the end of a lovely little avenue close under the château, watching Paris. The view pleased me, and they planted a chair for me not far behind themselves. If I had moved a little to the right I might have seen the Panthéon, but there the French could see me, and would probably fire upon me. While I drew, Prince Charles, the brother of the King, came up, and said that he had known the place for fifty-two years, and during all that time it had been a source of frequent pleasure to him. "What a pity! why burn it?" said he. One of his aides-de-camp suggested that it was merely because he, that is Napoleon, had lived in it. Another prince looked over my shoulder. His name I have forgotten, but I remember that either he or one with him stepped knee-deep in the little conduit that trickled down the avenue, and that one of his aides-de-camp, seeing a whip lying at my side, picked it up, and tapping his boot with it, said, "Aha! a souvenir of St. Cloud." My newly-made friend, the lieutenant in command, told him it belonged to me, and had never been Napoleon's, and of course he and every one else were convulsed with laughter.

THE EXODUS FROM ST. CLOUD.

It was on my way to Meudon that I met a motley train of poor people coming from St. Cloud, turned out of house and home, not to make room for the Prussians, but for their own safety. St. Cloud has been constantly under fire, and to stay there was to risk one's life. A brother and sister, old bachelor and old maid, with their *bonne* and *gouvernante*, led the dismal procession. Some of them were doubtless on their way to quarter themselves upon more fortunate friends; but others, I fear, knew not where they would lay their heads that night, being only too glad to get out of the range of their countrymen's guns.

FRANCE, 1870.

A NIGHT AT THE FRONT.

It was pitch dark now, and sentinels had got very vicious, shouting their "Halt!" and "Wer da?" and advancing their bayonets in a most threatening manner; and when we gained the high road, and knew our way, and asked permission to continue it to Versailles, were advised strongly to go no further. It was hinted that we should be certainly arrested, probably bayoneted, and possibly shot. We were very wet and wretched; but our lives were still dear to us, and we accepted the kind invitation of an officer to stay the night at his post. The name of the place was Le Restaurant à la ferme de Bruyères, and our host was lieutenant of the 7th King's Grenadiers. He gave us a hearty welcome, bread without cheese in a lordly dish, not Sèvres this time, but British porcelain Minton; good red wine in plenty, and, last of all, hot whisky toddy. Was not this enough to warm the heart of us, and make us of a cheerful countenance, cold and miserable though we were? Then he led us to our chamber. It wasn't spacious; it was not hung with Gobelin tapestry. We had, however, lots of hay, blankets, and pillows, but only one mattress. This we placed longways with the hay at the foot, and when the host had helped us make our bed, and we had exchanged "Good night" for "Gute Nacht," we lay down, three in a bed, myself in the middle, flanked on each side by a British officer, and soon the British snore, as national as the British cheer, declared that Her Majesty's officers slept.

A CAVE BARRACK IN THE PARK OF ST. CLOUD.

I was indebted to a soldier, who was kind enough to arrest me, for a sight of one of the quaintest barracks that, I suppose, ever held soldiers; for, having explained who I was, not only did the officer at once order my release, but he invited me to his quarters, of whose picturesqueness he was very proud. Fancy a cave cut in the lime-stone, closed by a door, with a toy figure stuck on one side, and a diary chalked on the other. He led me through this into the ante-room, a long, dark chamber, whose low roof of heavy blocks of stones was propped up with two or three saplings. On either side mattresses were laid, leaving a narrow path between. Most were occupied by soldiers, some asleep, some sitting up and grinding coffee, others cutting tobacco; and others furbishing their arms. A light glimmered at the farther end, and I went on, and passing under a rude archway, entered the inner cavern the quarters of the officers. The atmosphere was rather catacomb-like. The furniture was magnificent, being, in fact, the spoils of the *Pavillon*, the little summer-box of the Emperor close by. Imperial candelabra glittered on an Imperial card-table, which the officers had just been turning to its proper purpose. Imperial vases of Sèvres china, one of them broken; wine and cognac bottles stamped with the Imperial (Ⓝ); two boxes of *chassepot* cartridges, beek, bread, a box of most delicious sweetmeats, half a shell, that had burst outside the cave, made up the motley burden of the table; while against it leant a *chassepot*, which, with the cartridges, had been taken from a French soldier made prisoner the night before. I remained with my kind hosts all night, but must confess I was not sorry when a streak of light stole into the cave, and told us it was morning.

Drawing of a visit to the grave at the Redancourt was traudes under the favor of
M.rs Vo[...]. — Monday Oct.r 10, 1870
Radin with food in [...] bag with [...] bottles, some milk, a little, whey
Noble [...] pitched [...] Captain [...] keep in in complies?

[...] Camp for boy Rad[...] and away him [...] that [...]
[...] Course of an after Gra[...] Oct.r 2 1[...]

[...] [...] [...]

FRANCE, 1870.

THE RUE DE L'EGLISE.

THE other day I made a pilgrimage to St. Cloud: I cannot describe how utterly destroyed it is. Hardly a house remains untouched, and very many are mere chaotic masses, not one stone standing on another. The Rue Royale looked like a long glacier of fallen stones and rubbish. The dark figures of three German soldiers returning from a search for wine in the cellars under the ruins wound their way amongst the heaps. At the corner over the shattered doorway of a gutted house was, "Chambre meublée à louer présentement." Down the Rue d'Orléans, opposite the hospital, there lay the wreck of a fire-engine and its hose. The Rue de l'Eglise, I think, was the very centre of the ruins. I sat down on the top of a pile of stones as high as the ceiling of the first floor, just opposite to No. 34, where there was a tablet, "Sapeur Pompier," attached. Before me a whole house had fallen in, except the party wall, on which were traceable the outlines of the various floors and rooms. On the second floor was attached a hanging kitchen with all its appurtenances complete: plates and saucepans on the stove, over it a frying-pan, a gridiron, three handirons, and at the side a little box for matches. There they all hung, as if nothing had happened. On the third story, pinned to a flake of tottering wall, was an almanac, and above that a row of hat-pegs. Flags of torn, discoloured papering dangled in the wind. In a house opposite, a flower-pot kept its place on the sill of a smoke-stained window; and at the end of this vista of blackened ruins stood the church, white, uninjured, shining in the sun. A thread of people kept passing along the gorge—I can't call it a street,—some looking for their houses, and others trying to save a remnant of their furniture. A woman had fixed a ladder against a window some way down, and was throwing bundles of salvage to her friends below. As they passed me I fancied they looked as if it were cruel in me to sit there quietly depicting their misery. "It is a fine picture, is it not, Monsieur?" some said bitterly. "Beau, mais triste," I replied, which reconciled them a little to me. The poor woman who had once lived in the room where the kitchen stove still hung in the air stood by my side in tears and pointed to it. "That is all that is left me," sobbed she, looking up at the suspended frying-pan.

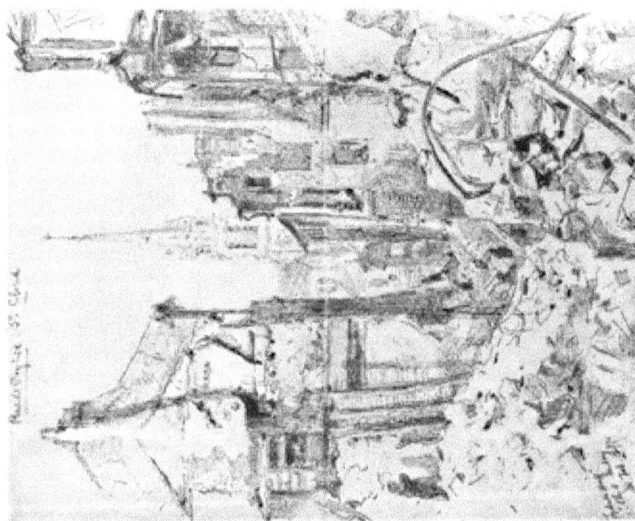

FRANCE, 1870.

SHROUD OF WHITE SAND.

A CAPTAIN of the German Feld Telegraph, a gentleman to whom I owe a great deal, lent me one day a horse and an orderly, and we rode to the scene of the fighting at Petit Bicêtre. One battle-field is very like another. There are the horses knocked about with shell; the trees in shreds, or hewn down and thrown across the roads, which are ploughed with shot or thrown up, to destroy their use; the fields strewn with *débris*. Dead horses here and there, while in the ditches men lie buried—scarcely buried,—with two twigs made into a cross for headstones, and on them stuck a slip of paper, with the name inscribed, to be washed or blown away by the first gust of wind or rain. The helmet of the soldier is placed on the mound, recalling the grave of Elpenor, and the epitaph:—

τῷ καὶ ζωὸς ἔρεσσον ἰὼν μετ' ἐμοῖς ἑτάροισιν.—Od. xi. 78.

Not far from Petit Bicêtre, near Petit Plessis, on a bit of heath-land, where tufts of heather cropped from a loamy soil, at a spot marked by a slender cross of the above description, five French soldiers lay lightly covered with the sand. Perhaps the wind had blown some of it away, but the covering was so slight and insufficient that each figure lay distinct in form, while the boots, peaks of *képis*, and here and there a bit of the dress, protruded from the insufficient shroud.

THE REVERIE.

THE officer to whom my visit in the Palace of Versailles was paid was, oddly enough, the brother of the soldier who was making the sketch of Mont Valérien from the branches of the chestnut-tree,—a subject I had made into a drawing for the *Graphic* a day or two previously.

I found him contemplating the picture of the First Consul crossing the Alps, evidently in a *rêverie*, in which the glories of the First Empire had a part. Some books and flowers, and pictures were by his bed-side, the gift of Mr. Home, the spiritualist, who spends a good deal of his time with the wounded here. My officer was shot in the leg at the affair of Bougival, and fell with no less than six bullet holes through his clothes. Here I found him cheerful—I hope, recovering; for he and his brother sufferers (there are several officers in the same room) are well attended to by a Sister of Charity—chubby, smiling, ever ready,—who flits about from one to the other, in a noiseless, unobtrusive way, the beau ideal of a nurse.

A scene and a visit in the Palace of Versailles

FRANCE, 1870.

"ONCE MORE IN THE SUNSHINE."

AFTER a reverie, should the sun and wind be warm, the convalescents would be moved through the big windows opening to the floor on to the broad balcony sheltered by the wings of the palace. Here their friends would visit them, sitting at the bed-foot, chatting or reading to them; and from there they could look across the broad park, the *char embourbé* of the sun, the still fountains, the statue of the Fighting Gladiator (I don't know if the Dying Gladiator is there), and the leaves that fell one by one on to the *tapis vert*, gradually leaving the bunches of mistletoe alone upon the tree-tops.

THE CROWN PRINCE VISITING THE WOUNDED.

SOMETIMES, too, as they lay in the saloons of the palace looking up at the pictures that blazoned the glories of France, now half covered up with planks, not to hide, but to protect them, the loneliness of officers and men would be relieved by a visit from no less a friend than the Crown Prince himself. I was present on one of these occasions, sitting in a corner making the sketches you see, but I had to retire. When I showed them to the Crown Prince and Princess on their visit to Sandown, Isle of Wight, in the summer of 1874, the Prince recollected seeing me in the corner. I did not remind His Royal Highness that he had me turned out.

Roumania and the Borderland. Edward Stefani at Venice...

The Crown Prince visiting the wounded in the palace at Venice.
Sept 20. 1890.

FRANCE, 1870.

THE THEATRE OF WAR.

Down the dark narrow passage where jolly crowds had hustled for a front seat in the pit—"a cockpit" now. Heavens! what a hideous sight! What a sickening stench! I cannot bear it. I go back; then try again. In the middle of the long room is a table, covered with rags and doctors' stuff, close to a fire, round which crouch those who are only slightly wounded. There is the long, low stage, with its far-drawn vista of ins and outs and nooks and corners, from which just the ends of straw beds and mattresses, mixed up with all the litter of the stage—lanterns, boxes, scenery, and dresses; the tawdry proscenium and half-dropped curtain; the gilded balcony over the orchestra, where lie wounded men, three on either side of the steps, one, nearly naked, binding up his own leg; the tiers of boxes at the sides, with their tinsel decorations and purple drapery, and under them the long foul line of wretches, some dying, some crying out at the touch of the surgeon, some desperate, with faces buried in their straw, praying, perhaps, for death; the play-bills and manager's notices still pasted over their heads, one, that " Les consommations doivent être payées en les servant," another, " Par ordre de police il est expressément défendu de fumer dans la salle." In the foreground is a group cowering round the stove, whose chimney pierces the arched ceiling by a hole, through which peeps one solitary little bit of pure blue sky. How they must have lain and longed for that pure sky, those wretched inmates of the loathsome lazarette! One victim was carried past me dead as I stood there, his clay-cold feet cropping from the cloth thrown round him. This is le Théâtre de la Guerre, and here is the epilogue! Here are some of those who " sought a bubble reputation even at the cannon's mouth." I have looked for Heroism in war, and found only Horrors. Pah! I am glad to get away; and, passing by the ticket-place and corps, I stand once more in the pure air and the sunshine.

FRANCE, 1870.

IN BATTERY No. 19 BEFORE PARIS.

I FIND on the back of sketches sent to the *Graphic* these notes :—

"I was in battery No. 19, before Issy all day before yesterday morning under fire. To-morrow I shall send two-page sketch of bombardment."

"I have just sent sketch, and you will find I have put nothing into the picture which I have not seen."

"Captain Müller's portrait. Captain Müller invented carriage for gun used. He took me into the battery. I shall get a description of it from him."

"They say the forts are occupied to-day. If so, I try to get in."

"N.B.—Châlet and apple-tree knocked about by shot."

"Sling for carrying shell to breech of gun by two men."

"The *tree* of earth, splinters, &c., thrown up by bursting shell."

"Fort d'Issy, with casernes burnt. Trees, with lower branches lopped away."

"The gun after firing, recoiling, and ducking."

"Man shovelling earth from the front of muzzle of gun."

"We lunched in the shell-room off cold turkey and claret, and while there a shell fell, and burst in the battery. It burst so that the base was left entire. We put this down *hot* between us, and made a stand of it for our claret-bottle."

THREE MILES FROM THE FRONT.

Who would draw when he could skate? Out of my window I can see le Bassin de Neptune. Will the ice bear? Of course it will. There go the burly Prussians down a stunning slide. I throw down my pencil and rush off by a short cut into the park, plunge down the bank, and take a header into the fountain. The ice is about two feet thick. There are just two holes in it—one for watering the Prussian guard at the gate, another for the frozen-out swans to paddle in. *En route* I call on Neptune, stand face to face with the god, grasp his trident, then slide away and up the bank again by the plank up and down which the swans used to waddle. At the end of the avenue we come upon the Bassin d'Apollon. How cold all the statues look, don't they, with nothing on but epaulettes and crowns of snow? Now we stand upon the brink of the canal. What a jolly scene—just three miles from the front! The snow mouffled white, the sky blue, fading into primrose, the trees all frosted, every twig and spray, their white tops dazzling white in the sun. Then on the ice—what a Vanity Fair!—a crowd of dark figures weaving a mazy dance as swallows do in some sheltered nook on a sunny but windy day. On the bank are old women with stalls with hot wine and cognac for sale, and lads with skates of a homely make. We miss the good old English screw at the heel, and feel we need much French *abandon* to trust ourselves to these. Yet we allow ourselves to be shod, and in a twinkling are winding amongst the crowd. What a nuisance those little sledges are that Prussian soldiers and French *gamins* force along with two goads that star and fret all the ice! Nuisance No. 2.—Those bigger sledges, that are pushed. Then these ranges of snowy mountains that the lounging sweepers will not remove. Then Valérien, the moment you try the outside edge backwards, fires a booming shot, that reverberates along the whole canal, shakes the frost-spray from the branches, and throws you off your balance. While you are sitting on the ice, criticize your companions. Notice the Frenchman yonder, got up in green, with pork-pie hat and embroidered jacket: he can't do anything, and yet how elegantly he does it! What poetry of motion! What affectation of pose! Now mark this long Prussian General, swinging along with tremendous strokes on running skates, with blades like yataghans; or that Bavarian Uhlan, who jumps, twirls, and whirls in the air, and on both edges, flinging his legs about like the arms of some raving cuttle-fish. Contrast them with the quiet style of the American, who, hands in his pockets, cuts marvellous figures in a space about the size of a dollar, a gentleman whose centre of gravity is entirely at his beck and call. Get up now, and be broomed over by *le petit balayeur*, when he has finished that green hussar. Here come two ladies, one English, the other American, sailing along like ships. One says she thinks that every gun sounds louder and nearer, and that the French will take Versailles; the other that she believes Paris is about to fall, because all the sparrows, wise birds, seem to have left it, and come to Versailles. So we talk three miles from the front. So we skate while Paris is bombarded. Look at this speck of red on skates—a little English child, though she lisps French as well as English. Dear little gap-tooth, jolly little round, red holly-berry! How her red petticoat and furred hood warm up the cold landscape and our cold hearts! How the German family-men look after her, and are set a thinking on the little girls they've left behind them, just her age—eight next birthday.

A wonderfully philoprogenitive people, the Germans! Bugbear after bugbear, booted, spurred, sword begirt, bends low and begs to lead her for a space. The biggest bugbear of all, a baron and a cuirassier, in a moment of ecstatic philoprogenitiveness, lifts her high in the air, lets her tiny feet and skates dangle for an instant, then deposits her again without a word of explanation. Her big brother, about as tall as a jack-boot, is too intent on wriggling backwards to demand any.

FRANCE, 1870-71.

THE LAST BIVOUAC.

We passed a group of some fifty dead arranged in five rows. Many of their poses were beautiful, most were horrible, all were awful. Some with uplifted arms, some pressing them to their sides as if still clasping musket at support, one tearing the handkerchief from his neck. The faces that were not blackened or bloodstained seemed more livid in the ghostly light. Above them shone the stars. They used to say that the spirits of the dead became stars.

I met heaps of people coming back from the Sèvres barricade—respectable husbands, with three or four bâtons of bread under one arm and a ring loaf over the other shoulder; decent wives, laden with baskets of provisions. Fancy meeting English tradesmen and their wives on their way back to Cheapside, after a tramp to Peckham Rye bastion barricade to fetch white bread from Norwood! The Sèvres bridge, you know, is broken down, but a temporary wooden planking spanned the fallen arch. The barricade made a lively picture. I had no sooner got through it myself than I turned sharp round and made this sketch, in spite of a persuasive nudge from a Prussian soldier to go at once and get my *laisser-passer* visé'd. But I could not resist the sketch. There were Prussian officers looking on at the corner, some sitting on the bridge. There were the privates with fixed bayonets guiding and directing the mob. It seemed to me that discipline was a little relaxed. I observed one of these privates taking toll—"*just a kiss and nothing more*"—from a damsel he had let through to fetch two loaves of bread, and the officers winked at it. Then, too, they winked at the little boys that crept under the *chevaux de frise* and darted back with this or that for a friend. I was amused at a nonchalant Frenchman, who, leaning between two arms of the *chevaux de frise*, with cigarette in mouth and hands covering ears, stood calmly smiling at the scene. He had not a *laisser-passer*, and did not want one apparently. Dogs went through unchallenged—a privilege they had earned by escaping the spit. One of these nondescript *chiens de chasse* looked bewildered at the new world suddenly laid open to him. Perhaps he hardly recognised it, it was so changed by ruin.

FUNERAL OF GERMANS IN FRENCH GROUND.

I followed a funeral the other day, when an officer and two of his men were buried. Behind the officer's bier walked a comrade, bearing on a velvet cushion the dead man's iron cross. It was an honour which had come to him the day he was buried, and he never knew that one item of his funeral pomp would be that prized decoration "for valour" for which he had so bravely striven. Then followed his general and brother officers, the Lutheran clergyman, and that band of mourners who had lost a comrade and a brother from out of their family, marching with steady step, their bayonets gleaming, to the swell of the "Dead March," alternating with the roll of the muffled drum. Frenchmen uncovered as the procession passed, doing reverent honour to their enemy in the presence of death.

It was evening before we reached the cemetery outside the town; the darkness was gradually covering the sky, and the mists were as gradually creeping along the ground to lend additional solemnity to the ceremony. There was a great mound of earth here, thrown out of the hole where lay in a common grave so many brave men. A strange contrast that. The great gaunt pit, with its mound of earth and a bare pole stuck in it, and the pretty white tombs of the people of Versailles hung with beads and decorated with flowers, statuettes, and immortelles. The land ceased, the chief mourners stood upon the fresh-turned mound, looking down into the grave, as the clergyman pronounced the funeral oration over the three dead men. Then the French gravediggers lowered the coffins into the pit, the earth rattled on the lids, there was a clash as the soldiers presented arms; the band struck up, and the men marched homewards once more. The parting volley over the grave was not given. The dead officer was of the 6th Regiment, and had received his wound in the action at Bougival. He was not on service that day, but had begged permission to join the fight.

Passing the barricade at Stähl's bridge. "Taking Toll" just a kiss and nothing more!

That Gott face Kriang and Vaterland!

FRANCE, 1871.

A SOUVENIR OF 1793.

ACCOMPANIED by a friend, an Indian officer, I ventured on a stroll along the Boulevards while the ferment occasioned by the German occupation was at its height. There are soldiers of all sorts who never salute an officer. The first thing we should do in their army reform would be to sew up their pockets. Next to the soldiers, the newspaper-vendors and ballad-singers are the most numerous. Most of the former are boys, wriggling in and out of the crowd, shrieking all the names of the new journals—"*Le Mot d'Ordre! V'là le Mot d'Ordre! Le Cri du Peuple! V'là le Cri du Peuple! Le Vengeur! V'là le Vengeur!*" *Vox Populi, vox Dei.* Look at the caricatures displayed in the shops—filthy many of them, most of them without wit. We only meet with them as we go farther in the Boulevards, not this side of Boulevard Poissonnière. In Goupil's window there is a picture in charcoal of two children killed together by a shell fallen in Paris. It is called 'Le moment psychologique,' the effects of bombarding in the nick of time. There is a crowd round the window craving to look at this and other clever sketches of scenes during the siege. I wonder what Citizen Doré has been doing these last four months—Citizen is a National Guard. There is a photograph here at the corner of an actress as Liberty. Liberty is extremely ugly, and in a white classic robe, reminding one of Demoiselle Candeille as the Goddess of Reason in 1793. Besides all the play-bills on the pillars there are notices and proclamations, begging the people to assume an attitude of dignity while the Prussians soiled Paris with their presence. At the end of the Boulevard St. Martin there is a crowd round an unfinished shop. It is a peep-show, and a National Guard is the showman: "Entrez, Mesdames; Entrez, Messieurs." There is an automaton figure, a Mumbo Jumbo, at the man's right hand, with black face and Turco costume. At the word of command, he beats the rappel, turns his head from side to side, and rolls the whites of his eyes horribly. Behind the man is a big canvas, with "Un Souvenir de 1793, et Charlotte Corday," in large letters. The edge of the pavement is lined with men and women and children selling wares of all sorts, many of the men in uniform. The Boulevard is a little market. It seemed to me that some were selling old arms not merely as curiosities. In the middle of the streets there were groups round orators or tumblers.

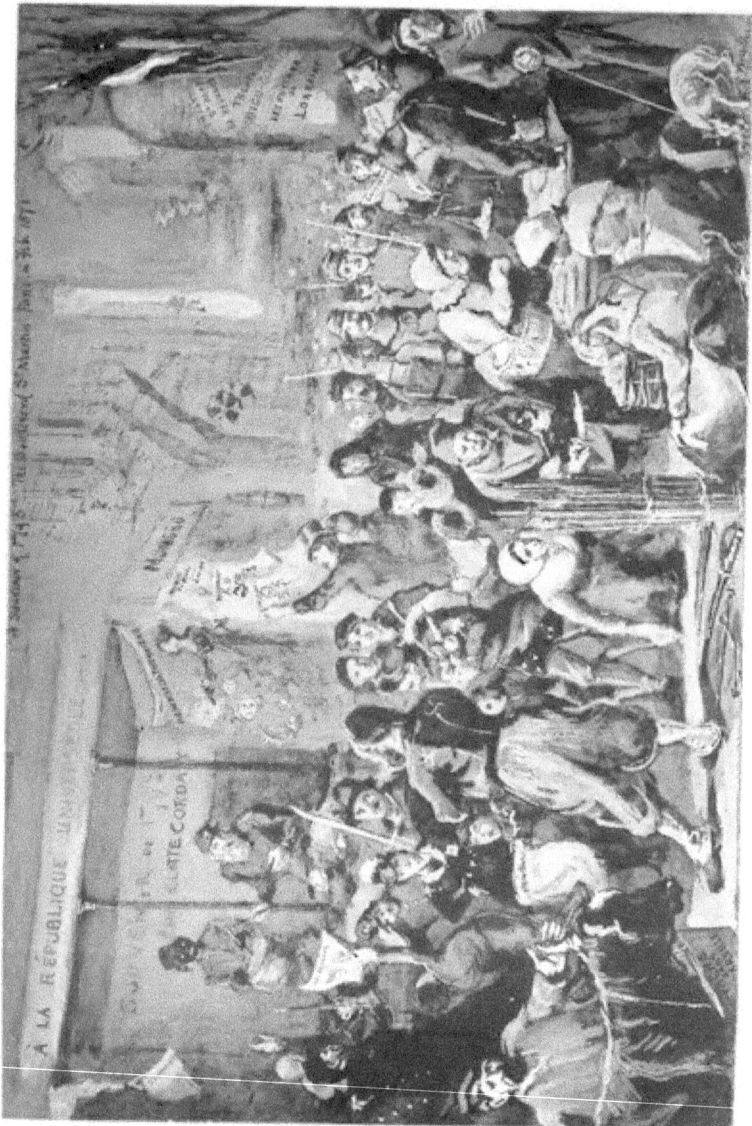

FRANCE, 1871.

A BENCH IN THE CHAMPS ÉLYSÉES DURING THE GERMAN OCCUPATION.

On my way back to the Place de la Concorde I passed several groups of soldiers, *billets* in hand, talking to the *concierges* of splendid houses. There is a rotunda in the Champs Élysées, and the Bavarians had bivouacked round it. There was a trench all round, and under its cover they had rigged up their kettles on cross-pieces of wood to boil their coffee. They were surrounded by a crowd of French men and women, peering at them over one another's shoulders with intense curiosity. I stopped opposite a bench decorated, perhaps, as it had never been before, and, as the French would say, as it never will be again,—with the lances of Bavarian Uhlans. Their pennants are light-blue and white, and stood tastefully arrayed by accident. On the bench lolled the Uhlans themselves in the easiest of poses, in green with red facings, with steel epaulettes, and white horsehair plumes, fan-shaped, down to the eye. Cords were drawn from tree to tree, and their horses were attached, those nearest nibbling the bark of the trees, which would long retain the German brand. It made a picturesque scene. The sun shone bright, and the French looked on with hands in pockets as usual; the Uhlans lounged, basked in the sunshine, and drank their wine.

AVENGED.

On Friday, the 3rd of March, 1871, the Germans evacuated Paris, and the exit was even more imposing than their entry. The road under the Arc de Triomphe, which had been purposely blocked up by the Parisians, was carefully levelled, and regiment after regiment passed through, cheering as they distinguished the names of the various German towns once conquered by that great enemy of their ancestors, Napoleon I., and which were now waiting to accord a hearty welcome to the men who had wreaked such an overpowering vengeance on the descendants of their victors.

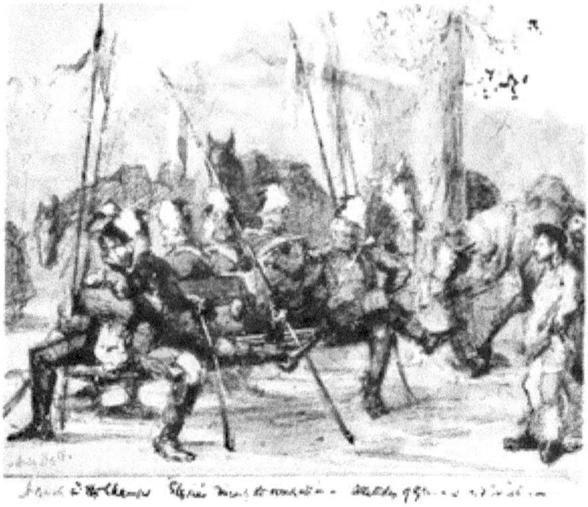

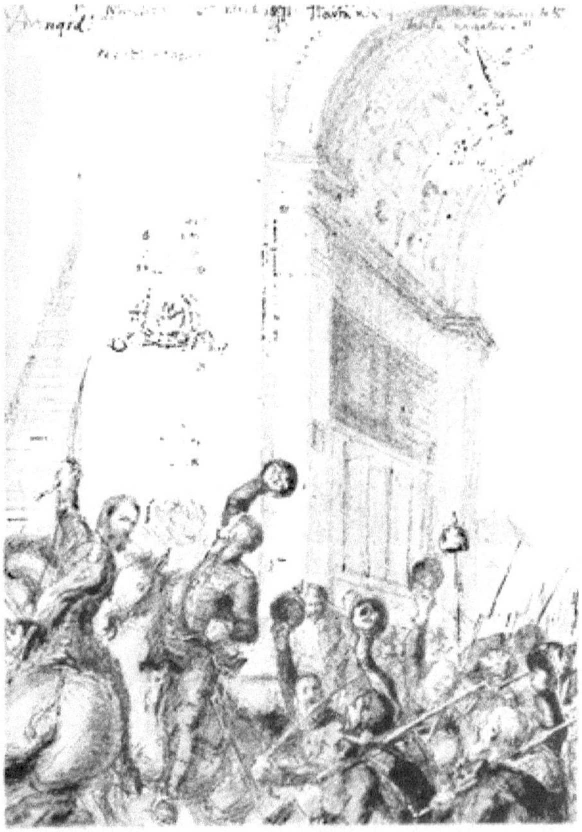

NAPLES, 1872.

VESUVIUS FROM POMPEII.

So this is Pompeii! Here the forum, and here the amphitheatre, and here shops with their appurtenances, and houses whose walls are covered with still vivid frescoes, all buried once, but now exhumed to look up again at the power that buried them—Vesuvius in its fury. If there be a demon genius in the mountain, what thinks he, as he rises with outspread wings over the city that he destroyed? These streets and houses are familiar to him. Shall he bury them again, or shall he turn and bury Naples?

UP THE CRATER OF VESUVIUS.

SUDDENLY the mountain, which had been still as death, awoke again, and threw up a pine-tree cloud. "Only ashes, Signore," said the guide, and we buckled to for the ascent. I find it impossible any longer to refuse the strap, and I cease to kick against the pressure from behind. In good sooth the ashes are getting tremendously deep, and the ascent awfully steep, and I am floundering about like a cat on the ice with walnut-shells on her paws. I flounder in spite of the fellows about me, whose assistance I affect to despise. Still I keep them on, because I can't help it, and because it makes an odd picture. Perhaps, after all, they helped me more than I am inclined to own. I put my feet in the tracks of the man in front, you know, and once or twice hung on like grim death to the straps. We kept stopping for breathers, and faced the wind as horses do after a gallop. I tried an orange, but, like the forbidden fruit, it turned to ashes in my mouth. I kept peeping up at the dense smoke whirled from the crater, getting uncomfortably near, slowly as we approached it. Then sometimes we put on desperate spurts to cross hot currents of sulphurous air. My boots by this time were full of ashes, and I longed, too late, for wellingtons.

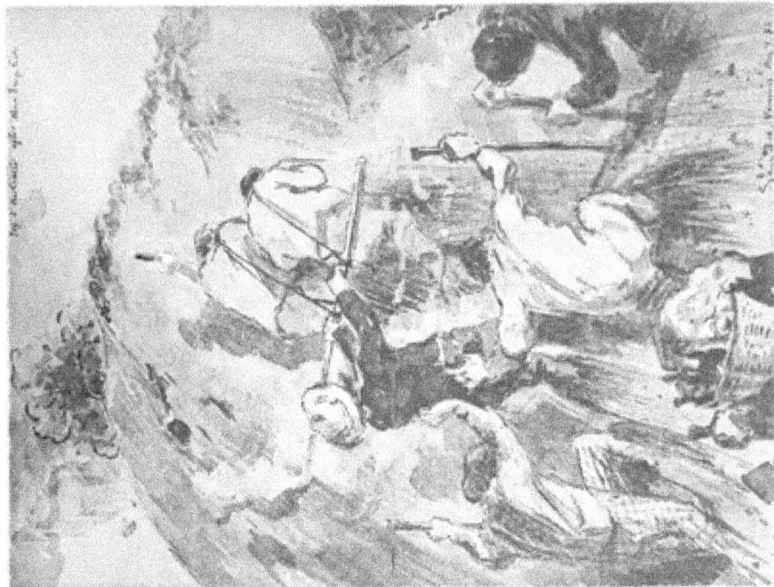

ROME, 1872.

ROME: ON THE STEPS OF ST. PETER'S.

"Per Carità, Signore."

Somehow or other in Rome one is always going up steps. If you go to St. Peter's you must mount the steps, and on the steps, alas! you must run the gauntlet of beggars. You may try to tack about, and try to avoid them by a zig-zag course, but they will catch you. You approach with composure one of the granite milestones that encircle the steps, seeing no beggar there; but behold! from the stone emerges a humpbacked witch, who twitches your elbow with her crooked hand, and, walk as you may, keeps up with you, and hands you on to the next. This time it is an old man, or a young one with a wooden leg. Now you have three upon you, and in a moment half a dozen. You cannot help noticing some of their hands twisted by long use into saucers for catching *soldi*. They surround you, almost stifle you with their cries, "Per carità, signore. Datemi un soldo, signore." What are you to do? "Scramble some coppers," is the happy thought that suggests itself to you, "and watch the cripples tussle on the ground." Over their heads you see others nimbly leaping down the steps. What are you to do? Run! run for the door of St. Peter's, and meet a beggar there holding up the screen for you! What annoys me most is the stolidity of their begging. They don't beg, they demand, and they thrust their hands in front of you, just as the elephant presents his trunk, with an expression of eye exactly like his, that says plainly, "Now, then, don't you see my trunk? Are you going to give, or are you not?" And yet I owe some thanks to the beggars of St. Peter's, for two of them made me capital models just on the brow of the steps, while the hot December sun played down upon us where "Issa l'Arabe di Gerusalemme sells trinkets and photographs." Hadn't I a crowd round me? But Issa l'Arabe did his best to keep them off, lent me his chair, and begged me to pay him a visit, and draw him for himself in his native costume.

HOLY STAIRCASE IN HOLY WEEK.

From St. Peter's we go to the Lateran, and from beggars to penitents. All have seen the Scala Santa, or seen pictures of it, like that called "Pilgrims at the Scala Santa," for instance. But in Holy Week the Holy Staircase becomes holier still. At the top of the stairs is placed a recumbent figure of Christ on the Cross, illuminated by candles at the head. And this the penitents, ascending the steps upon their knees, and approaching in the same fashion, kiss reverentially, laying their alms on the cloth on which the figure lies.

Before I dared to sketch the solemn, and yet somewhat comic scene, I invoked the protection of St. Luke, my patron saint, who, tradition says, painted the portrait of the Saviour in the "Sanctum Sanctorum" just behind where I stood.

ROME, 1872.

IN LIMBO PENT.

Do you see what they are doing there—those imps from the Inferno, with heads of monsters—a cock, a skull, a devil, and a Bismarck? There's an unfortunate priest in the middle of them, "in limbo pent." Whoop! Hi diddle diddle, the priest's in the middle! Round and round they go, such jolly dogs are they, till the priest grows giddy. "We know you, we know you by your red nose: you are a Papalino." Bah!—it is only a Carnival freak.

THE ODOUR OF SANCTITY.

AND then when the ceremony was over (it was Candlemas Day in St. Peter's, 1872), when they had returned each with his sanctified candles to their stalls, incense was wafted from the swinging censer of the acolyte, who bowed profoundly before them. The thin films of the incense crept in and amongst them, and wove imaginary halos round their heads as the *odour of sanctity* was wafted abroad. There was perhaps amongst them a Leo X., sensuous as Raphael has painted him; a Hildebrand, perhaps, who would humiliate some future Italian king; an honest ascetic, like Adrian VI., and may be a Nicholas Brakespeare, who would crush, if he could, some reformer like Arnold of Brescia, and perhaps there was not.

"IN QUESTO FENT" MADRID. ... ... Leonard 1853

ROME, 1872.

THE FESTIVAL OF THE BEFANA.

THERE is a sort of Feast of Trumpets in honour of the Befana (corruption of Epiphany), who is a good fairy, and brings all sorts of presents for children, and puts them in the stalls near the Pantheon, trumpets especially. We went in rather a strong party, and as we neared the scene of action our ears were saluted with such a squealing, squalling, and trumpeting, that we thought we were close to a pandemonium rather than a pantheon. The crowd thickens as we advance; we crush and squeeze through it, and defend the drums of our ears from impertinent trumpets as best we can. Then we determine to retaliate; there is no help for it, so we arm ourselves, some with trumpets, some with whistling clay figures, caricatures, maybe, of noted men. . . . . Look at these two with inflated cheeks and spouts of trumpets for mouths, making their faces like masks of ancient comedy! There are Satyrs, Fauns, an English Syrinx at my elbow (her name is changed, alas! though not to *Reed*), and perhaps the great god Pan alive again amongst us. Here is a Faun blowing on a double pipe like an antique bas-relief! Sometimes a shadow falls across our heads, and we look up and fancy some great vampire is hovering over us. It is a paper harlequin, with legs and arms gesticulating furiously, borne aloft by some merry grig below. We make way politely—everybody crushes and is crushed. It is no good hating the profane vulgar, or resenting a nudge. Though we had been squeezed enough in an hour, this Saturnalia still went on with unabated vigour, and we woke up in the night to hear the street below us resounding with trumpets.

REVIEW BEFORE PRINCE HUMBERT IN THE PIAZZA DEL POPOLO.

A REVIEW in the Piazza del Popolo, before the Crown Prince of Italy, under the Pincian, crowded with spectators. The troops, Romans clad in the garb of Gaul, no longer ancient Romans with spear, and shield, and sandals, march round the obelisk that stood before the Temple of the Sun at Heliopolis, and was brought to Rome by Augustus, under the Pincian, where Belisarius encamped during the siege by Vitiges, and not far from the Porta Pinciana, where, tradition says, Belisarius begged: "Date obolum Belisario."

EXTREME UNCTION.

I WAS standing one afternoon on the steps of S. Maria Maggiore just after sunset, my errand being to inquire affectionately after a purse, lost, as I believed, in the same church on Christmas Day. I asked for the sacristan, and the people told me he was away, and pointed to a procession slowly wending its way to a house down a neighbouring street. They were carrying the Holy Sacrament to some one dying. Boys with candles walked in pairs before the priests who carried the Host. Over it was held a *baldacchino*, and the sacristan walked by the side of the priests. The rite was soon finished, and the procession returned to the church and entered it while we stood with uncovered heads. Then we followed them through the dim light of the basilica into a chapel, where mass was said, the boys with their candles kneeling and forming a semicircle at the foot of the steps of the altar. Behind them were indistinct figures *in reverential poses*; but the boys were not much impressed, and improved the hour by vigorously scratching their Italian heads.

ROME, 1872.

A PUBLIC LETTER-WRITER.

I am led by my cicerone, Mr. Keeley Halswelle, and planted opposite a big umbrella of varied hue, under which, in black shade, sits a little old man at a little old table. He is one of the public letter-writers (*scrivani publici*). Don't you see his pen, and ink-pot, and sand-tray, and his shells and bits of marble for paper-weights? What a world of wisdom there is in his face? No wonder; he is surcharged with the affairs of tribes of *contadini*: he writes their love letters and their business letters, and altogether knows more of their secrets than any confessor. What a lot of comediettas are enacted before these tables! Here an Italian Sam Weller, more unlettered than the original Sam, dictates his billet-doux to his Italian Mary, while Signor Veller corrects and suggests portentously. Here a faun, like Pan, with shaggy goatskin thighs, whispers his secret passion for some Syrinx to the reeds of the *scrivano*, too low for some old busybody to catch. What, can none of them read or write? Don't they know their A, B, C, nor even their S. P. Q. R.? Not one; those "*Avvisi*" and "*Notificazioni*" over the umbrella are all hieroglyphics to them, and they are in blissful ignorance of their future erudition heralded in that notice, "Istruzione Publica." Public instruction, indeed! There is need of it.

SHAVING DOGS ON THE STEPS OF TRINITÀ DE' MONTI.

"In the good old time," that's just a month ago, before they cleansed the steps to the Piazza di Spagna, you could not descend them without stopping before a very curious spectacle. You halted at a line of dogs tied to the stonework in the sun, some shivering, some dripping, some dozing, some restless. Dogs they are,—poodles, *lupetti Maltesi*,—but jolly dogs no longer, and they look up at you with the most woe-begone expression. "Yes, sir," they seem to say, "you may well look at us. We are indeed objects of pity, deprived of coat, fleas, and liberty. The hand of Fate has been upon us; Fate, in the person of that old woman with a pair of scissors, has ruthlessly washed and shaved us. If you have a heart, pray, oh pray to the Dog-star to temper the wind to the shorn poodle." You turn to the old woman, and find her bending low over a poodle patient, who lies under her scissors as if under chloroform.

Queer old lady that! I sketched her the other day in the very act. At first she showed a coy reserve, a maiden modesty, and retired behind a slab. But I stood my ground, and time being valuable to her (Heaven knows how many dogs she shaved a-day!) she reappeared, and set to work again. So did I; and in the midst of it she looked up, fixed me with her eye, smiled, and pointed to her mouth. I took the hint, and left an offering, before I went, on the altar beside the victim. And what a philosophic victim! Nothing of the Cynic about him, but the complete Stoic. He never snarls or flinches; he lies there perfectly resigned, turning his eyes up as he ponders why poodles of all the dogs in the world should be allowed to wear hair only round the head, the stump or tip of the tail, and in anklets above the feet.

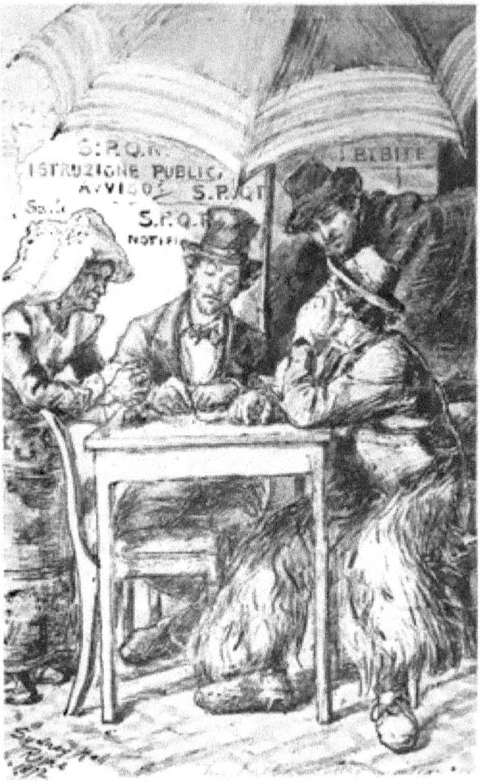
S.P.Q.R.
ISTRUZIONE PUBLIC
AVVISO
S.P.Q.R.
S.P.Q.R.
NOTIFI
BIBITE

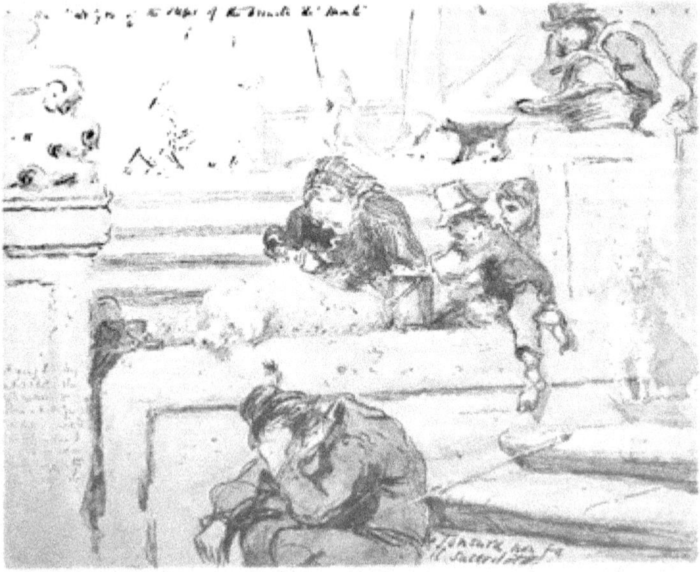

ROME, 1872.

"THE LAST TARANTELLA."

THE steps of the Trinità de' Monti are, or rather used to be, sacred not only to the old woman who shaves and washes dogs there, but also to the tribe of models employed by the numerous artists resident in Rome. Christs, Madonnas, Satans, heroes, heroines, and brigands, even *Il Padre Eterno*, if one may say so without being profane, were found here posed magnificently, or basking in the sun, while *fanciulli* of all sizes played about, and *bambini*, models from their very birth, were bred and almost born upon the steps. Below there lay the Piazza di Spagna, the haunts of *forestieri*, picture-buyers, and above the Church of the Trinità de' Monti, and in it the Descent from the Cross, by Daniele da Volterra, so that they seemed a link between the world of those who come and go and buy below, and a world above of religion and art. But they were destined to be *improved off*, and the *tarantella* I saw them dance in Carnival time, 1872, was perhaps their last upon the steps. Even then a *sergent de ville* lowered down upon them from behind, emblem of the sword, or rather broom, impending over them.

ENGLAND, 1872.

"ENFANTS DE LA PATRIE."

As I marched along listlessly on the road to Bottle-Dash-Down, during the autumn manœuvres, 1872, I could not help thinking of my countrymen, the "Northerners," as these invaders call them. I pictured to myself the volunteers,—

> " Marching along,
> Half a score strong,
> Great-hearted gentlemen, singing this song,
> "God for Sir Charles." *
> Sir John † and his carles
> To the Devil, that sent them their treasonous parles."

I lagged behind my column for a while, and was caught up by a battery of Royal Artillery. They halted, and then I got my subject, "Enfants de la patrie." Of course the children of Tarrant Gunville came to look at the gun, and the gunners sat motionless, and looked grimly at the Gunvillers. Both the children and the bronzed, shaggy veterans were "Enfants de la patrie."

* Sir Charles Stavely.   † Sir John Michell.

ENGLAND, 1872.

WONDERFUL SAGACITY OF A CART-HORSE, AND CIVILIANS PREPARING TO RECEIVE THE ENEMY.

How it rained! We had to stand it, we had no umbrellas; but the civilians squatted behind theirs, and ducked behind the shelter trenches, now prepared to resist "cats and dogs." I have heard of a people who periodically went out to fight the north wind, and of another who declared war with the sun; but these good folks battled with the rain, and pluckily too, ladies and all. Yet, sir, they are a confounded, terrible nuisance at manœuvres. And if they will come and see them, let them have balloons at the Government's expense, and then we shall have the ground clear. They came in ponderous waggon-loads to see the fighting; they dashed fearlessly through barricades and crossed blown-up bridges. But in one case a horse, with a waggon-load behind him, stopped short at the foot of a bridge labelled "Undermined." Marvellous sagacity in the common cart-horse! I mentioned the circumstance to a distinguished veterinary surgeon, and he was inclined to think it was the weight of the waggon-load and the ascent of the bridge that stopped the horse, and not the printed notice "Undermined." He had heard of a learned pig, but never of a horse that could read. I am not sure about that.

BRIDGE
UNDERMINED

Sydney Wolf

Wonderful widening of opacity — a mman Cart-horse ! Shout of (applause).

S.K.

The [...] of Brighton Parking Scene —
[...] Clouds [...]

ENGLAND, 1872.

PARTANT POUR LE SALISBURY PLAIN.

"OMNIA VINCIT AMOR."

My road lay past a line of huts devoted to married soldiers. At the door children romped and made mud-pies, and mothers stood nursing smaller children. I wondered if I had ever seen one of those matrons as a neat nursemaid in the park, with the soldier-sweetheart and neglected perambulator by her side. Over each door was a number; could it mean the number of inmates, or families, or children in each family? Probably the last.

None seemed to believe in the imminent deadly war. Even now, when regiments were starting for the front; wives taking leave of their husbands. Yet all, including the women, shared in this spell of incredulity. They believed it was a report got up by the newspapers. "Good-bye," said a soldier to his wife, with a child in her arms. "Good-bye, old gal; I'm off to meet the henemy." "What henemy?" she said, rudely. "Why, them as has invaded Hingland," rejoined her husband sadly. "Tell that to the marines!" she exclaimed. Now there were no marines stationed in Aldershot; so this was impossible.

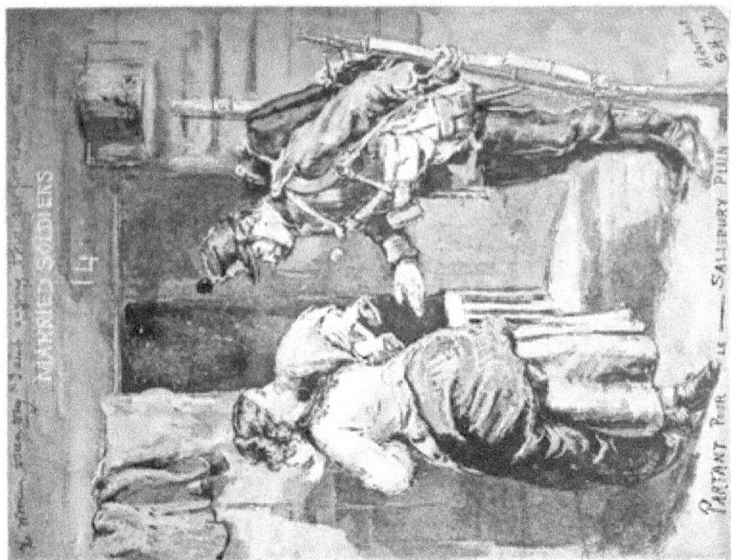

Sydney Hall

ENGLAND, 1872.

NOT A BIT KILLED OR WOUNDED.

THE sketch is a little like *The Last Bivouac*, only the prostrate men are not a bit killed or wounded. It has been a piping hot day in Blandford Camp during the Autumn Manœuvres of 1872, and tired soldiers are basking or sleeping in the sun; perhaps some have drunk a little too much to the tune of,—

> " And let me the canakin clink, clink!
> And let me the canakin clink !
> A soldier's a man,
> And life's but a span,
> Why then let a soldier drink."

THE BAKERIES.

THESE bakeries are worth your notice; the ovens are like steam hearses. They are attached to waggons which will hold everything a baker wants for making bread with the exception of bone-dust, alum, and potatoes. *Pat-a-cake, pat-a-cake, baker's man*, says Staff-Sergeant Brookhouse, Sir John Michell's chief baker; and *so they do*, certainly, *as fast as they can*. Then the kneaders throw each loaf to a middle-man, who says "*up*," and throws it to a third, who lets it down, picks it up again, and puts it on to the "peel," dirt and all. Then the "peeler" shoves it into the oven. Each oven bakes enough for a thousand men a day. German yeast is not employed at the bakeries. This is wonderful, when we consider that all other in-stitutions of the camp have been remodelled on the German system.

WATER TANKS.

THE first thing a general thinks of in pitching a camp is water. A regular old soldier told me this yesterday. Now on these wavy downs where is the water? There is one well, which they would soon draw dry, and there is a pond close railed in and inviolable as a font of holy water. Where do they get it then? They pump it up, sir. They pump it up, two hundred feet, from Monkton to the valley through which runs the little river Tarrent. There they have a donkey-engine of some horse-power, which fills that line of tanks you see on the hill. Of course I sketch them, though they are ugly enough.

Not all Killed or Wounded " by Sydney Hall

The Water Hawks in Race Course Street "

THE RHINE, 1874.

"A SHARP CORNER."

ON the Rhine there are no sharp corners until the boat has passed Ehrenbreitstein, the Gibraltar of the Rhine; after this pilots are taken on board in succession, who know a particular reach of the river. The pilot himself lends a hand to the wheel, and he is helped by two or more of the ordinary crew. The captain meanwhile is passive, and sits in the midst of action calmly smoking a very long cigar. The men's figures are thrown in the shade by the circular awning over their heads. On this side of the river the sun streams down upon the rocks terraced with vines, and crowned with old castles. The other side of the gorge is in dark shade. Where the rocks converge the nearest a cannon is fired, upon which the startled ladies occasionally throw themselves into the arms of the nearest gentlemen.

BÂLE, 1874.

THE FERRY-BOAT.

WE leave the Rhine at Bingen to see it again at Bâle. But how changed! How it rushes under the bridge! There are quaint balconies on its bank that remind one of Metz, or the Tiber, though its colour is not yellow, but hoary white—milk-and-water colour. There is just time to sketch a bit of it, with those tall poplars on the opposite bank, and the ferry-boat that the stream carries backwards and forwards across.

LUCERNE, 1874.

THORWALDSEN'S LION.

To go and see the Lion, because we must do it, is irritating, but inevitable. There he is; what do you think of him? No dog of Landseer ever was so anthropomorphic; you might fancy you heard him sob. The little pool beneath him seems to have gathered from his tears.

> The tears ran down his cheeks so fast,
> They made a little pond at last.

There was once a Swiss guard who tended him, but his shade now rests only in photographers' windows. Who is, who was, this Swiss guard? Does he live to tell the tale of the 10th of August, 1792, to peasants from Sempach and Schwyz, who cannot translate the Latin inscription?

RUSSIA, 1874.

"TURNED OUT TO LET THE CORTÉGE PASS," AND "THE EMPEROR'S PRIZE."

NEVER to be forgotten is February 18th, 1874, the day of the bear-hunt given in honour of the Emperor of Austria. How we went by train to *Mallaya Vischera*, and slept in the carriages—we, I mean, who were outsiders; how the waiting-room at Vischera was fitted out with tents for the Emperor and the Princes; and how I was figged out for the occasion.

If it wasn't cold, why, it ought to have been: so over a thick coat heavy with astrakan I put an enormous shuba; over goloshes I managed to pull high boots of sheepskin, with the wool inside. It was difficult for me to walk even on the level platform before we started in sledges for Gatchina.

Ugh! the sledges! A hundred miles in a limber waggon with friend Furley over the broken-up roads in France was tramway-travelling compared with them! Such jolting, bumping, pitching, floundering! The peasants stood barcheaded to let the big line of the cortége file by. Sometimes we met their sledges, and then they would have to turn out into the deep snow to let us pass. The sledge would ride upon the surface; the pony would sink up to the girths, and the faces of the sheepskin-clad girls who drove would expand into a smile as far as their tight bright kerchiefs would allow.

The glorious snow-laden woods where we stopped for the rendezvous! No Christmas-tree in a toy-shop in London can give you any idea of the snow on the branches. It seemed as if the discharge of a gun would bring all those snow cupolas and cornices down upon us. The Royal hunters stood placed at equal intervals along a narrow path stamped in the snow. Though the guest of the day was the Emperor of Austria, I thought Englishmen would be more desirous to know how their own Prince of Wales shot, so I determined to ask leave to stand by him.

It was difficult for me, accoutred as I was, to move in the deep narrow snow groove. I managed to scrape by the Emperor, who stared at me drolly. The Prince too looked in wonder as I approached; may be I wasn't so very unlike the bear. The snow was sucking my outer boots off: they had never been really on my feet, my heels were now in the calves of the legs of them. The feet splayed out like the paddles of a seal. It grew harder and harder to waddle on. I had a petition to make, and was very nervous about it. It was the first time I had spoken to His Royal Highness. My speech was at length composed, and when fairly near enough, I summoned all my courage and my breath, and said in a loud, firm voice: "Would Your Royal Highness allow— "

"Hush! for God's sake; we expect the bear."

The bear came, and the Emperor shot it, and four men bore off the Emperor's prize.

www.ingramcontent.com/pod-product-compliance
Lightning Source LLC
Chambersburg PA
CBHW030620270326
41927CB00007B/1261